Note to Parents and Teachers

The READING ABOUT: STARTERS series introduces key science vocabulary and concepts to young children while encouraging them to discover and understand the world around them. The series works as a set of graded readers in three levels.

LEVEL 3: READ ALONE follows guidelines set out in the National Curriculum for Year 3 in schools. These books can be read alone or as part of guided or group reading. Each book has three sections:

• Information pages that introduce key concepts. Key words appear in bold for easy recognition on pages where the related science concepts are explained.
• A lively story that recalls this vocabulary and encourages children to use these words when they talk and write.
• A quiz asks children to look back and recall what they have read.

CRANES, SCALES and SEESAWS looks at BALANCING. Below are some answers and activities related to the questions on the information spreads that parents, carers and teachers can use to discuss and develop further ideas and concepts:

p. 7 *What other animals need to balance well?* Ask children to list animals in groups, e.g. forest animals, mountain animals, minibeasts. Encourage them to watch wildlife: squirrels, cats and birds all use their tail to help them balance.

p. 9 *What happens if you push a domino over?* When one domino falls over it knocks over the next one, which pushes over the one after that, and so on. Ask children to think of other objects with a narrow base that fall over easily, e.g. skittles.

p. 11 *How could you use a lump of clay to make the pencil pot balance better?* If you put a lump of clay into the bottom of a pencil pot, it will balance better.

p. 13 *What do you think happens if you try to tip the straw over?* Because most of the toy's weight is at the bottom, it will not fall over. When you try to tip it, it stands upright again. This is why a bus has its engine low down, to stop it from tipping over.

p. 15 *Why shouldn't you stand up in a small boat?* When you sit down in a boat, all the weight is low down, so the boat is steady. But when you stand up, you move your weight higher up, and it is easy to tip the boat over.

p. 17 *How could you balance three coins against one on a seesaw?* You need to move the three coins even closer to the middle. You could even balance four or five coins against one by moving them closer and closer to the point where the seesaw balances.

p. 22 *What do you think happens when a top stops spinning?* It falls over!

ADVISORY TEAM

Educational Consultant
Andrea Bright – Science Co-ordinator, Trafalgar Junior School, Twickenham

Literacy Consultant
Jackie Holderness – former Senior Lecturer in Primary Education, Westminster Institute, Oxford Brookes University

Series Consultants
Anne Fussell – Early Years Teacher and University Tutor, Westminster Institute, Oxford Brookes University

David Fussell – C.Chem., FRSC

CONTENTS

4   Balance

6   Weight

8   A Wide Base

10   Heavy and Light

12   Tilting and Tipping

14   On the Water

16   Seesaws

18   Scales and Cranes

20   High Up

22   Wheels, Wings and Rotors

24   Story: I'm Joining the Circus!
      Pat wants to become an acrobat,
      but can she learn how to balance?

31   Quiz

32   Index

© Aladdin Books Ltd 2007

Designed and produced by
Aladdin Books Ltd
2/3 Fitzroy Mews
London W1T 6DF

First published in 2007
in Great Britain
by Franklin Watts
338 Euston Road
London NW1 3BH

Franklin Watts Australia
Level 17/207 Kent Street
Sydney NSW 2000

Franklin Watts is a division of
Hachette Children's Books.

ISBN 978 0 7496 6876 1 (H'bk)
ISBN 978 0 7496 7597 4 (P'bk)

A catalogue record for this
book is available from the
British Library.

Dewey Classification:
531

Printed in Malaysia
All rights reserved

Editor: Sally Hewitt

Thanks to:
The pupils of Trafalgar
Infants School, Twickenham, for
appearing as models in this book.

Photocredits:
*l-left, r-right, b-bottom, t-top,
c-centre, m-middle*
All photos istockphoto.com
except: Cover tl, 5br, 19t — Jim
Pipe. Cover tr, 22ml — Digital
Vision. 2tl, 6tr, 7tl & mr, 8mr,
9tr, 11tr & tl, 17m, 18b, 21bl,
31tr — Marc Arundale / Select
Pictures. 2bl, 20tr — Comstock.
3, 4t, 8b, 23tl, 31bc — Corbis.
5tl, 12b — Courtesy Scania. 5bl,
7ml — Ingram Publishing. 12tr,
31ml — Courtesy John Deere.
15bl, 26ml — Photodisc. 21mr
— John Foxx. 22b — Courtesy
US Navy. 29tr — Select Pictures.

BALANCING

Cranes, Scales and Seesaws

by Jim Pipe

Aladdin/Watts

London • Sydney

Surf-board

BALANCE

This man is **balancing**
on a surf-board.
Balancing means standing
up without falling over.

We can **balance** our bodies.
So can animals.

Look at this flamingo.
It can sleep while
balancing on one leg!

Flamingo

We can **balance** an object too.
We can make it more steady.
See how all these objects **balance** well.

Tent
Objects with a wide
base balance well,
like this teepee.

Bus
It is hard for a bus to
tip over because it is
heavy at the bottom.

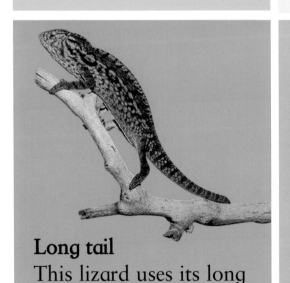

Long tail
This lizard uses its long
tail to keep its balance.

Crane
A crane uses heavy
weights to balance
it when it is lifting.

WEIGHT

When you try to walk in a very straight line, you use your sense of balance.

If too much of your **weight** moves to one side, you lose your balance and fall down.

Some people can balance on their head or their hands!

Handstand

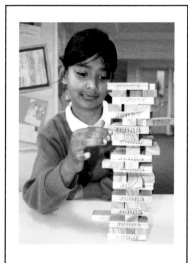

In this game, too much weight on one side makes the tower fall over.

This boy is balancing a book on his head.

This girl is balancing an apple on her hand.

This man is balancing a ball on his head.

Which of these is easiest to balance? Which is hardest?

A kangaroo uses its tail to help it balance when it runs.

What other animals need to balance well? Think of animals that live in trees and on mountains.

A WIDE BASE

Try balancing your body. If you stand
on one leg, you soon start to wobble.
It is easier to balance on two feet.

On one leg

On your hands and knees,
you touch the floor in
four places. This **wide base**
makes you very steady.

Things that have a **wide base**
balance well. A pyramid
is a very steady shape.

Pyramid

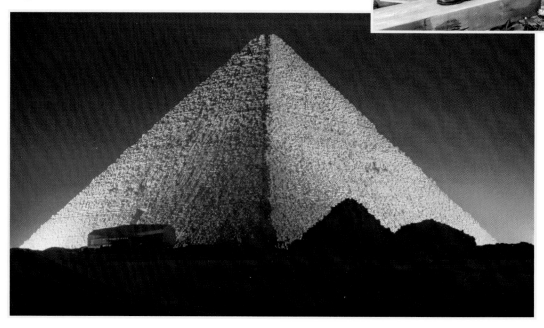

8

These dominoes are standing on their ends. They have a narrow base.

What happens if you push one over?

A bicycle has two wheels. It has a narrow base. When you get on, it is hard to balance.

A tricycle has three wheels. It has a **wider base**. It is much easier to balance.

Tricycle   **Bicycle**

HEAVY AND LIGHT

Light objects are easy to tip
over. It is easy to knock
over a house of cards.

Heavy objects need a hard
push to tip them over.

Things balance best when
they are heavy at the bottom.
Heavy pots stop tall
plants from falling over.

Plant pots

Does an object balance better if you make it heavier? A bottle half full of sand is harder to tip over than an empty bottle.

Sand

But when you put a **heavy** lump of clay on top of an empty bottle, it tips over easily.

So you need to add the weight to the bottom of an object to help it balance.

Pencil pot

When you put lots of pencils in a pot, it can tip over.

How could you use a lump of clay to make the pot balance better?

TILTING
AND TIPPING

When something leans over, we say it **tilts**. Sometimes a bus needs to **tilt** a little bit, but it must not fall over.

A bus or truck that is heavy at the bottom balances well.

Passengers must not stand on the top floor of a bus. Why not?

A digger's weight is low down to keep it steady. Its two legs spread the weight wide.

Tilt test

Racing car

Look at this racing car.
It is very close to the ground.

All the car's weight is very low down.
This stops it from **tipping** over easily.

Make a wobbly toy. Ask an adult to cut a table tennis ball in half. Fill one half with clay then stick a straw into the clay. Now stick a paper figure to the straw.

What do you think happens if you try to tip the straw over?

ON THE WATER

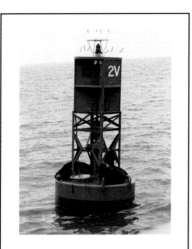

A buoy is heavy at the bottom to stop it tipping over.

A ship needs to be heavy at the bottom to balance well.

If a boat is too heavy on top, wind or **waves** can tip it over.

In the past, ships carried heavy rocks so they were heavy at the bottom.

Look at this ship. Can you see the heavy red **keel** that stops the ship from tipping over?

Ship

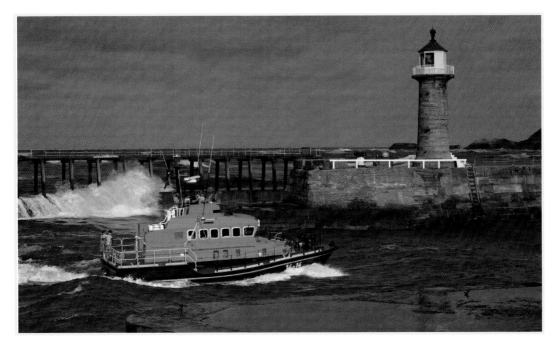

A lifeboat can stay upright
even in very stormy seas.

Lifeboat

A lifeboat is very heavy at the bottom.
If a big **wave** tips it over,
it spins the right way up again.

A wide boat balances
better in the water than a
narrow canoe. It also helps
if people sit in the middle.

Why shouldn't you stand
up in a small boat?

SEESAWS

These children are playing on a **seesaw**. There is one child at each end.

They balance each other, so it is easy to make the **seesaw** go up and down.

What would happen if there were two children at one end and only one at the other end?

The shapes on a hanging mobile balance each other.

Seesaw

This boy has made a **seesaw** using a ruler. With two coins on one end and one coin on the other, the **seesaw** tips over.

1 coin   2 coins

Balancing coins

When the boy moves the two coins nearer the middle of the **seesaw**, it balances!

Everything has a point where it balances. On a **seesaw**, this point is in the middle.

Make your own seesaw using a ruler and coins.

How could you balance three coins against one?

SCALES AND CRANES

Scales are like a seesaw. When its two sides weigh the same, the **scales** balance.

When one side is heavier, that side goes down.

Are bigger objects always heavier? Think about a tennis ball and a balloon. Which one weighs more?

Old scales use metal weights to weigh things.

Scales

18

Crane

Cranes pick up heavy loads and lift them into the air. A very heavy load could make a **crane** tip over like **scales**.

But a **crane** has heavy weights at the opposite end to help it balance.

Lots of other machines need to balance. The big arms on this fairground ride balance each other.

HIGH UP

Acrobats can walk along a tightrope, **high** above the ground.

The heavy pole helps them balance. It adds weight low down. If an acrobat tips over on one side, he lowers the pole on the other side.

Acrobats on a tightrope

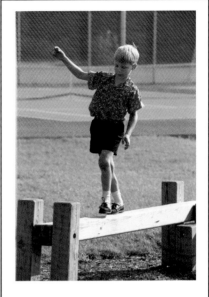

When you put out your arms, they help you to balance.

Monkey

Parrot

A monkey uses its tail when it climbs. When it tips to one side, the tail moves to the other side to keep its balance.

A parrot on a branch or **high** wire uses its tail to help it balance, too.

A potato is hard to balance on its end.

But if you stick two forks into the potato like this, it will balance!

The forks add weight low down.

WHEELS, WINGS AND ROTORS

When a **wheel** spins, it can help an object balance.
A bicycle is hard to balance when it is not moving.

When the **wheels** are moving, it is much easier to balance.

A spinning gyroscope can balance on a thin wire.

Cycling

When a top spins around and around, it balances on its end.

What do you think happens when it stops spinning?

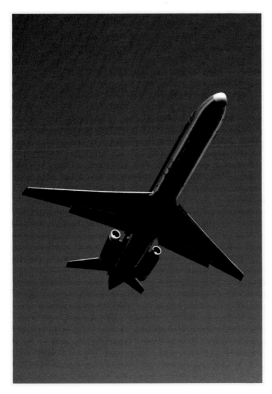

Plane

Flying objects also need to balance. Planes and birds need two **wings**, one on each side.

A helicopter has a big **rotor** to lift it into the air. But the **rotor** also makes a helicopter spin.

A helicopter needs a small **rotor** on its tail to stop it from spinning.

Helicopter

Rotors

I'M JOINING THE CIRCUS!

Look out for words to do with balancing.

Pat is very excited. She is going to the circus with her friends Paula and Danny.

They walk into the big stripy tent. "Our seats are up there," says Mum.

"Watch out," says Paula.
"These steps are steep."
"Hold onto the rail," says Pat.
"It helps you balance."

Bright lights come on.
Clowns rush into the ring.
One clown is riding a unicycle.

"Wow!" says Danny. "It must be hard to balance on one wheel!"

24

Pat loves the acrobats. She watches how they use their arms and legs to balance.

One acrobat stands on the end of a seesaw. His heavy friend jumps on the other end and makes him fly into the air!

One of the acrobats walks along a tightrope. He is high up in the air.

Mum is afraid he will fall. She can't look! "Don't worry," says Dad. "That pole helps him to keep his balance."

What a great show! After, Pat says, "I want to join the circus."

The next day, Pat goes to the park. "If I'm going to be an acrobat," she says, "I must learn how to balance."

Danny lends Pat his skateboard. "Take off your bag, first," says Dad.

"That heavy weight on your shoulders will make it hard to balance."

Pat begins to skate. But it isn't easy! She soon starts to wobble. "Help!" she cries.

"Don't keep your feet so close together," shouts Paula.

"Keep your feet apart. It will give you a wide base and help you balance," says Dad.

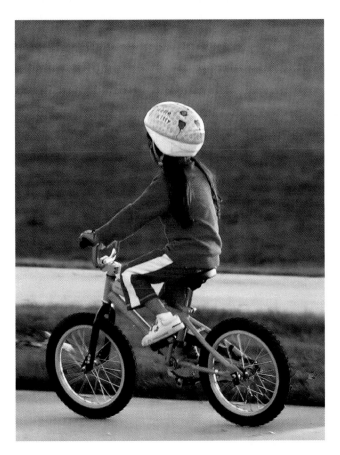

The next day they take turns riding on Paula's bicycle.

Paula has a go first. It looks easy. But when Pat gets on, she tips over.

"Try going faster," says Dad. "It's easier to balance when the wheels go around."

"I need more wheels," laughs Pat. "Two small wheels at the back will give my bicycle a wide base. It will be easier to balance."

"Don't worry, you will get better if you practise," says Danny.

The children walk over to the playground.
Pat and the others climb up the big spider's web.

"It's like being an acrobat on a tightrope!" says Paula.

Pat keeps her feet wide apart to help her balance. She hangs on tight with her hands.

They take turns to walk along a narrow beam. They use their arms to help them balance.

Some other children are playing on the roundabout. Pat and her friends join in.

"Hang on tight," says Dad.

"It's hard to balance on a roundabout when it spins around," says Pat. It makes her dizzy.

Pat has a rest then walks over to the seesaw.

Danny sits on one end. Andy sits on the other end.

"Can I sit behind you?" asks Pat.

"Are you sure?" asks Danny.

"Your weight and Danny's could make me shoot up into the air like that acrobat at the circus!" says Andy.

When they get home, Pat sees a squirrel in the garden.

It runs along a wire.
It jumps onto the tree.
Then it hangs upside down to drink from a water bottle.

"Its long tail helps it balance," says Dad.

"It's an acrobat," says Danny.

"It should join the circus with me!" laughs Pat.

WRITE YOUR OWN STORY about things that balance or draw a picture showing something or somebody losing their balance. Look around you and see how things balance. You can make a chart listing them.

Object	Wide base	Weight low down	Like seesaw	Tail
Tent	✓			
Skateboard	✓	✓		
Old Scales			✓	
Bird				✓
Tortoise	✓	✓		

QUIZ

What makes this tower fall over?
Which brick is safest to
remove so it will not fall over?

Answer on page 6

Can you think of two things
that help this digger to **balance**?
Why does it need to be steady?

Answer on page 12

How does a pole help a
tightrope walker **balance**?

Answer on page 20

What helps these objects balance?

Crane

Kangaroo

Pyramid

Buoy

Answers on pages 7, 8, 14, 19

INDEX

acrobats 20, 25

balance 4, 5
balancing your
  body 8
balls 7
beams 28
bicycles 9, 22, 27
bottles 11
buses 5, 12

cards 10
cranes 5, 19

diggers 12
dominoes 9

fairground
  rides 19
flamingoes 4

gyroscopes 22

handstands 6
heavy 10, 11

helicopters 23
high up 20, 21

kangaroos 7
keels 14

lifeboats 15
light 10
lizards 5

monkeys 21

parrots 21
pencil pots 11
planes 23
plant pots 10
pyramids 8

racing cars 13
rotors 23
roundabouts 29

scales 18
seesaws 16,
  17, 25, 29

ships 14, 15
skateboards 26
spinning 22
squirrels 30
surf-boards 4

tails 5, 21, 30
tents 5
tightropes 20
tilting 12
tipping 13
tops 22
towers 6
tricycles 9
unicycles 24

waves 14, 15
weight 6, 29
wheels 22, 26
wide base 5,
  8, 9, 26
wings 23
wobbling 13